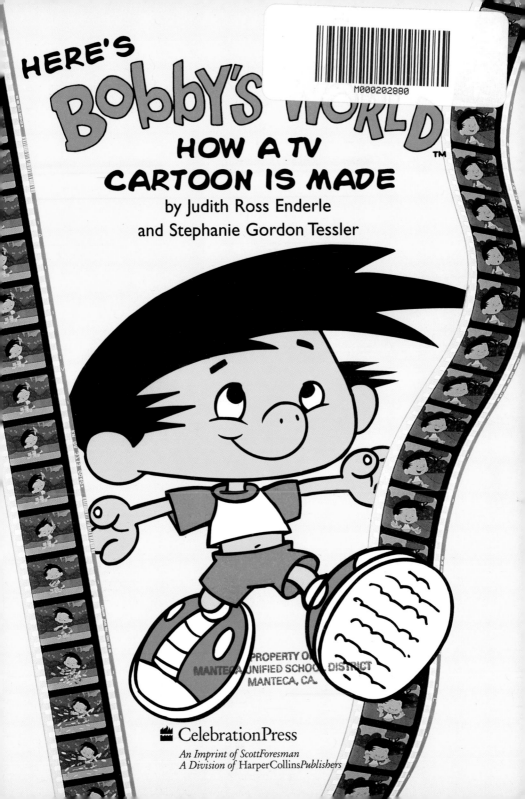

# HERE'S BOBBY'S WORLD™

## HOW A TV CARTOON IS MADE

by Judith Ross Enderle
and Stephanie Gordon Tessler

CelebrationPress

*An Imprint of ScottForesman*
*A Division of HarperCollinsPublishers*

**H**ere's Bobby! He's a TV cartoon star!

He's going to make the TV cartoon *Bobby's World.*

First stop is a brainstorming meeting. This is where Bobby gets lots of good story ideas. Some ideas come from things that happen to real kids.

**A**fter the meeting, writers and artists create a "show guide." This book tells everything about *Bobby's World*. It tells everyone who works on the show about Bobby, his family, his room, his dog Roger—everything!

**N**ow it's time to write scripts and draw models. Writers work on the scripts. A script is a story. It has all the words, actions, and sounds to make one *Bobby's World* cartoon.

**A**rtists draw models that show the *Bobby's World* cartoon characters looking surprised, sad, angry, or glad. They draw the characters standing up, sitting down, and turning right and left. Using model sheets, artists draw the *Bobby's World* characters the same way all the time.

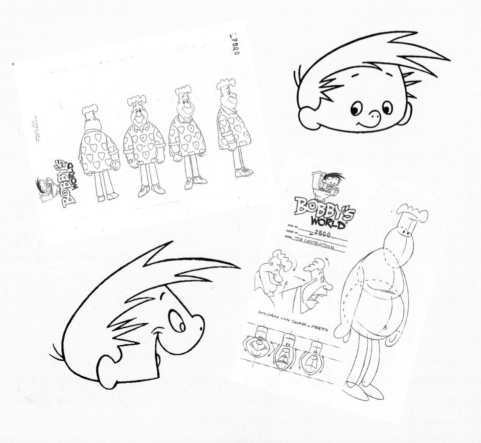

ext, artists draw storyboards to turn the script into pictures. Storyboards look like a *Bobby* comic book—with words, camera directions, and notes under each drawing.

Bobby picks the actors to record the voices of the cartoon characters. He chooses his friend Howie Mandel to be his voice. When the voiceover tape is finished, the cartoon drawings will be matched to the tape.

When the tapes are finished, words and actions are timed. Timing is written on exposure sheets. This shows how much film is needed to say each word. The sheets help match cartoon actions with the sound. Mouth sheets tell the artists how many mouth movements and shapes make up each word. Each movement is represented by a letter.

13

Using the storyboard as a map, some artists draw actions. Others draw props and costumes. These drawings are photocopied onto clear plastic sheets called cels.

Other artists paint background scenery to go behind the cels. Over 18,000 cels make up one cartoon.

**C**artoon cels are painted on the back. Each part of the drawing has a number showing what color to paint. The painters wear white gloves so they don't get the cels dirty.

# Roll-'em!

Putting drawings and sound together is the director's job. The director makes sure the cartoon is not too long or too short. Twenty-four frames make one second of film. Each cartoon covers thousands of feet of film.

19

When the film is ready, an editor checks that mouths and voices match. The editor uses a machine called a flatbed. Then music and sound effects are added, often with a computer.

ound is more than talking. It's noises like footsteps, ticking clocks, cat meows, stormy weather, songs, and bouncing balls. The person who creates the sound effects is called a foley artist. Many objects are used to make sound effects. Now the film is ready for everyone to see. It can go to final print.

**B**obby loves TV cartoons. He's going home to practice his drawing and his writing so he can make more *Bobby's World* cartoons.